FAMOUS NATIVE AMERICANS™

Sacajawea
Shoshone Trailblazer

Diane Shaughnessy
Jack Carpenter

The Rosen Publishing Group's
PowerKids Press™
New York

Published in 1997 by The Rosen Publishing Group, Inc.
29 East 21st Street, New York, NY 10010

First Edition

Book Design: Danielle Primiceri

Photo Credits: Cover, pp. 4, 16, 19, 20, 22 © Corbis-Bettmann; pp. 7, 8, 12 © Bettmann; pp. 10, 11 © Archive Photos; p. 15 © Richard Cummins/Corbis.

Diane Shaughnessy
    Sacajawea: Shoshone Princess / Diane Shaughnessy, Jack Carpenter.
        p.   cm. — (Famous Native Americans)
    Includes index.
    Summary: A biography of the Shoshoni Indian girl who served as interpreter, peacemaker, and guide for the Lewis and Clark Expedition to the Northwest in 1805–1806.
    ISBN 0-8239-5107-3
    1. Sacajawea, 1786–1884—Juvenile literature. 2. Lewis and Clark Expedition (1804–1806)—Juvenile literature. 3. Shoshoni Indians—Biography—Juvenile literature. [1. Sacajawea, 1786–1884. 2. Shoshoni Indians—Biography. 3. Indians of North America—Biography. 4. Women—Biography. 5. Lewis and Clark Expedition (1804–1806).] I. Title. II. Series.
F592.7.S123S53 1997
978'.004974'0092—dc21   97-17642
                                                                        CIP
                                                                         AC

Manufactured in the United States of America

Contents

The Shoshone

Sacajawea (sak-uh-jeh-WAY-uh) was born around 1788. She was the daughter of the chief of the western Shoshone (shuh-SHOW-nee) tribe of American Indians. The western Shoshone lived mainly in what is now Idaho, Utah, and Nevada, near the Rocky Mountains.

The Shoshone were a **nomadic** (no-MAD-ik) tribe. In order to find food, they moved when the seasons changed. They hunted buffalo and gathered roots, seeds, nuts, plants, and berries that grow in the mountains. As a girl, Sacajawea learned to find and pick these foods. She also learned how to live as a nomad.

As a child, Sacajawea learned to find food and to move from place to place.

5

Bird Woman

When Sacajawea was about ten years old, she was **captured** (KAP-cherd) by another tribe, the **Minnetarees** (min-ih-TAH-reez). She was taken more than 500 miles away, to work for a Minnetaree family. The Minnetarees lived in one place all year. They lived in round homes made from earth and grass. They farmed and grew their own food. Sacajawea learned to farm too. It is uncertain what she was called as a child, but she was given the name Sacajawea by the Minatarees. Sacajawea means "Bird Woman."

Some Native American tribes, such as the Shoshone, hunted and gathered their food. Others, such as the Minnetarees, grew their food. ▶

Sold to a Fur Trapper

About three years later, Sacajawea was sold to a French Canadian fur trapper. His name was **Toussaint Charbonneau** (too-SAHN SHAR-bun-no). Sacajawea was to work for Toussaint. But Toussaint soon married her. They had one son, **Jean Baptiste** (ZHUN bap-TEEST).

Toussaint wasn't kind to Sacajawea. He often yelled at her. Sometimes he hit her when he was angry.

◀ *Many settlers in the western part of North America followed the example of the Native Americans by trading or selling animal furs and skins.*

9

Lewis and Clark

In 1804, Sacajawea and her husband met Meriwether Lewis and William Clark, the leaders of the Lewis and Clark **Expedition** (ex-peh-DISH-un). Lewis and Clark were sent by President Thomas Jefferson to **explore**

Meriwether Lewis worked closely with President Jefferson. The president knew he could trust Lewis to do a good job.

William Clark was excited when his good friend, Meriwether Lewis, asked him to join his expedition. ▶

(ex-PLOR) the northwestern part of North America. They had set up camp with the Mandan Indian tribe for the winter. The Mandan lived near the Minnetarees, close to where Sacajawea and her husband lived.

Looking for Guides

Lewis and Clark learned that Toussaint was a fur trapper, and that he knew the northern part of the country well. They hired him as a **guide** (GYD) for their expedition. They asked Sacajawea to come too. Lewis and Clark knew that having a Native American woman along would help them show other Native Americans that they were peaceful. Sacajawea could speak several Indian languages, and knew the ways and **customs** (KUS-tumz) of many Native American tribes.

Sacajawea was a very good guide. She knew the land through which the expedition was traveling, how to live while traveling, and how to find food on their journey.

The Expedition

Sacajawea was a great help to the expedition. Because she was able to speak to many of the Indian tribes they met, she could help Lewis and Clark get horses and fresh supplies. And when the food ran out, Sacajawea knew where to find and how to cook roots, nuts, berries, and other plants that they could eat.

The expedition was headed toward the Rocky Mountains and Shoshone land. Sacajawea knew the land and was able to find the quickest way through the mountains.

Sacajawea led the Lewis and Clark Expedition across some of the most difficult land to cross in North America—the Rocky Mountains. ▶

Meeting Family

About four months into the **journey** (JER-nee), Sacajawea and the expedition met a group of Shoshone people. When Sacajawea began to interpret for Lewis and Clark, she realized that the chief of the group was her brother, **Cameahwait** (kam-ee-UH-wayt). She had found her family!

But rather than staying with her family, Sacajawea helped the explorers get the horses they needed. She finished the long journey with them, and returned to Fort Mandan.

Today, as in Sacajawea's time, family is very important to the Shoshone Indians. Sacajawea thought about staying with her family when she found them. But she knew that Lewis and Clark needed her to guide them back to Fort Mandan.

The Mystery

No one knows for sure what happened to Sacajawea after she returned from her journey. Many people think that she left her husband and traveled to St. Louis, Missouri. There she left her son, Jean Baptiste, with William Clark. Clark had offered to keep Jean Baptiste safe from Toussaint and to raise him as his own son.

Some people say that Sacajawea died at the age of 25 from a serious illness. But others, including the Shoshone, believe another story.

Sacajawea is an important part of American history. She is remembered in many ways. This statue of her ▶ is in Portland, Oregon.

Shoshone History

The Shoshone say that after the expedition, Sacajawea returned to the tribe and took the name **Porivo** (poh-REE-voh). Porivo married again and had several more children. She spoke French and knew a lot about the Lewis and Clark Expedition.

The expedition had opened the West to white **settlers** (SET-ul-erz). These settlers soon began to take Shoshone land. Porivo spoke out about the rights of the Shoshone to stay on their own land. Porivo lived to be 96 years old and died in 1884.

Many Shoshone believe that Sacajawea, or Porivo, tried to help the Shoshone keep their land safe from settlers.

Always Remembered

No matter which story is true, Sacajawea played an important part in the history of the United States. There are three mountains and two lakes named for her, and 23 **monuments** (MON-yoo-ments) were built in her honor. Because of her strength, courage, and **independence** (in-dee-PEN-dents), Sacajawea will always be remembered and honored.

Glossary

Cameahwait (kam-ee-UH-wayt) Sacajawea's brother.

capture (KAP-cher) To take by force.

custom (KUS-tum) The way a group of people does something.

expedition (ex-peh-DISH-un) A journey for a special reason.

explore (ex-PLOR) To travel over little-known land.

guide (GYD) Someone who is hired to lead other people somewhere.

independent (in-dee-PEN-dent) Thinking or acting for yourself.

Jean Baptiste (ZHUN bap-TEEST) Sacajawea's son.

journey (JER-nee) A long trip.

Minnetarees (min-ih-TAH-reez) An American Indian tribe.

monument (MON-yoo-ment) Something that is built in honor of someone or something.

nomadic (no-MAD-ik) When a person or group of people moves from place to place to find food.

Porivo (poh-REE-voh) A Shoshone woman that some believe was Sacajawea.

Sacajawea (sak-uh-jeh-WAY-uh) The Shoshone woman who was a guide for the Lewis and Clark Expedition.

settler (SET-ul-er) A person who moves to a new place and sets up house.

Shoshone (shuh-SHOW-nee) An American Indian tribe.

Toussaint Charbonneau (too-SAHN SHAR-bun-no) Sacajawea's husband.

Index

46649

DATE DUE
